THE BUSY
BODY BOOK

THE BUSY

BODY BOOK

A Kid's Guide to Fitness

Lizzy Rockwell

Dragonfly Books — New York

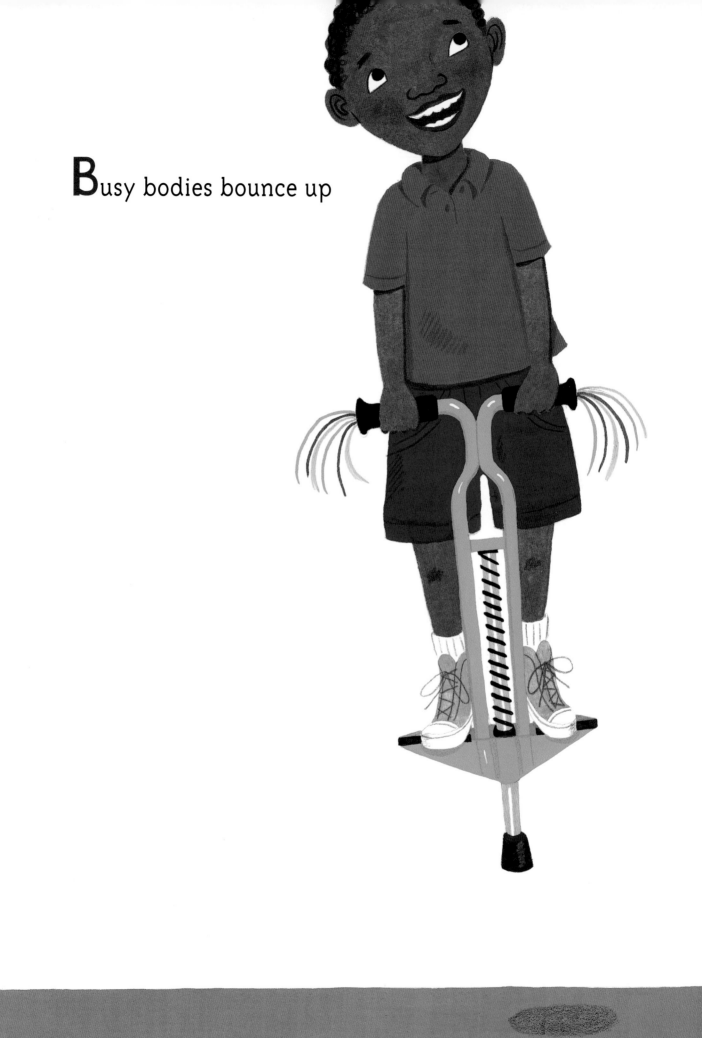

Busy bodies bounce up

and down.

They stretch from side to side and run all around.
They catch and throw. They push and pull.

They pedal, they paddle, they roller-skate, too.
When you get busy, what do you do?

Your body is meant to be busy. It's meant to move fast, lift heavy things, and walk or run for miles. Just look at it.

You have hands for clapping, feet for stamping, legs for leaping, and arms for swinging. You can jump, sprint, twist, and twirl.

You can do all that because your body is *built* to move. Underneath your skin is a strong, hard skeleton made of bones. Bones keep your body standing tall. Joints connect bones so you can bend.

THE SKELETON

You are made up of 206 bones.

The **skull** protects your brain.

Teeth are the only part of your skeleton that you can see.

The **spine** is made up of many small bones connected by joints so your back can bend and twist.

The **ball-and-socket joint** in your shoulder lets your arm move in a circle.

Hinge joint

Ribs protect your heart and lungs.

Ball-and-socket joint

The **thigh bone** is the longest bone in your body.

The **hinge joint** in your knee can bend back and forth.

Half of the bones in your body are in your feet and hands.

Muscles are attached to bones by tendons. Muscles let you move and lift and stretch. When you use your muscles again and again, they don't get worn out; instead, they get stronger.

THE MUSCLES

Tendons attach muscle to bone. You have more than 20 tendons in each wrist.

Facial muscles let you smile, blink, chew, and talk.

Ligament

Triceps help you push open a door.

Biceps help you lift heavy things.

Back and stomach muscles let you stand up straight.

Gluteus maximus is the large muscle on your bottom.

Quadriceps lift your leg and bend your knee when you walk.

The **Achilles tendon** attaches your calf muscle to your heel bone.

Ligaments wrap around muscles and tendons to hold them in place.

You have more than 630 muscles.

Inside your skull sits your incredible brain. Your brain
controls every move you make and thinks your thoughts.
It gets information about the world from your five senses.

Then it tells your muscles
what to do and how to move.
Messages travel back and forth,
at lightning speed, along wire-thin
fibers called nerves.

THE BRAIN & NERVES

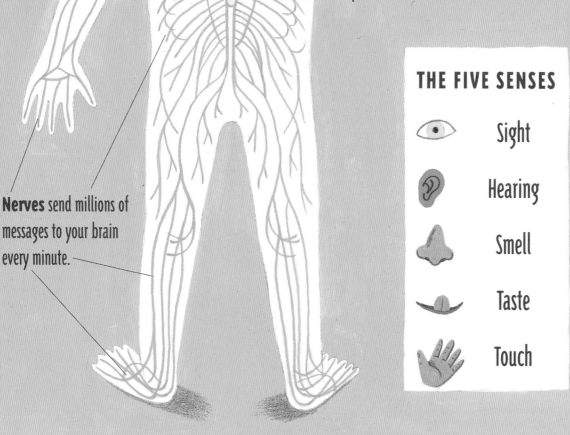

Your **brain** is made up of the cerebrum, cerebellum, and brain stem.

The **cerebrum** is the largest part of your brain. It controls most of your thoughts and movements.

The **cerebellum** controls balance and coordination.

The **brain stem** controls your heartbeat and breathing.

The **spinal cord** is protected inside your spine. It connects all other nerves to the brain.

Nerves send millions of messages to your brain every minute.

THE FIVE SENSES

Sight

Hearing

Smell

Taste

Touch

Your body is an amazing, living machine. And it only needs a few things to make it go.

Like air to breathe.

Food to eat.

And water to drink.

These things come into your body through your mouth or nose. But then where do they go and what do they do?

When you breathe, your lungs collect oxygen from the air. Your muscles need oxygen so they can move. Your brain needs oxygen so it can think. When you breathe in, you get fresh air. When you breathe out, you get rid of stale air.

THE LUNGS

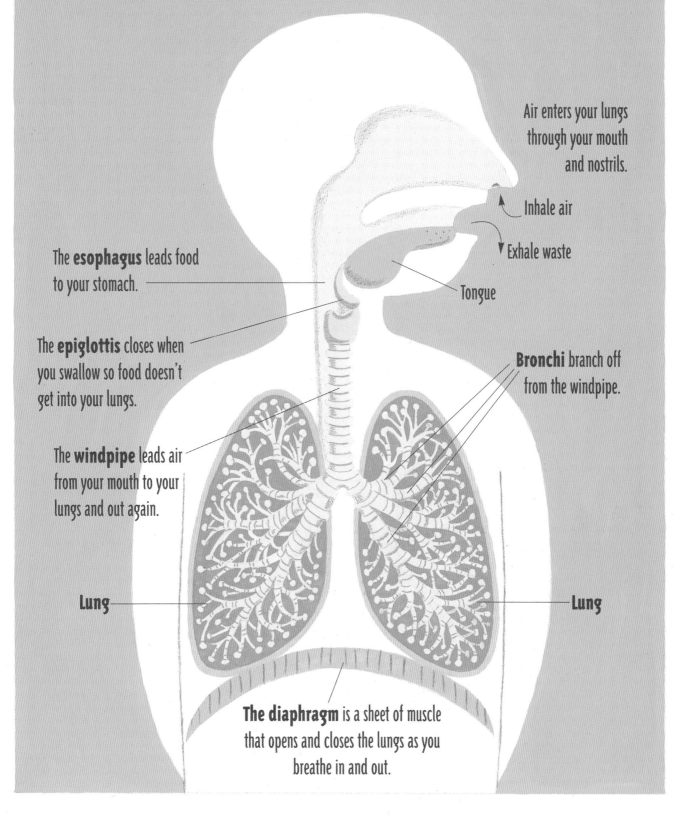

Air enters your lungs through your mouth and nostrils.

Inhale air

Exhale waste

The **esophagus** leads food to your stomach.

Tongue

The **epiglottis** closes when you swallow so food doesn't get into your lungs.

Bronchi branch off from the windpipe.

The **windpipe** leads air from your mouth to your lungs and out again.

Lung

Lung

The diaphragm is a sheet of muscle that opens and closes the lungs as you breathe in and out.

The heart moves oxygen from your lungs to the other parts of your body. Your heart pumps blood through long, thin tubes called vessels. The blood picks up oxygen in the lungs and carries it to your muscles and to your brain.

When your body gets busy, it uses more oxygen. Your heart beats faster and your lungs breathe deeper.

THE HEART & BLOOD VESSELS

Blood vessels carry blood in two different directions—away from and back to the heart and lungs.

The **heart** is the strongest muscle in your body. It beats more than 10,000 times a day.

Vessels in lungs pick up oxygen that has been inhaled and drop off waste to be exhaled.

Arteries (red) carry oxygen-rich blood from the lungs out to the body.

Veins (blue) carry oxygen-poor blood back to the lungs to be refreshed. Waste from blood is exhaled by the lungs.

Capillaries are tiny blood vessels that allow blood to reach every part of you.

Bone-Building Foods

Energy Foods

Muscle-Building Foods

As blood travels through your body, it also picks up food and water from the intestines. Then it delivers them where they are needed. Food gives your body energy. Your muscles use energy to move, your heart uses energy to pump, and your brain uses energy to think. Food also supplies the materials that build bone and muscle.

THE STOMACH & INTESTINES

Mouth grinds food and mixes it with saliva.

Esophagus pushes food down to your stomach.

Stomach churns food and mixes it with acid. Food becomes a thick liquid.

Small intestine absorbs tiny food particles through its spongy lining. Food enters the bloodstream.

Large intestine absorbs water and leads unused food parts out of your body when you use the bathroom.

All living things need water to survive. There is water in your muscles and around your brain. It is the main ingredient in your saliva, sweat, urine, and blood.

Because your blood is mostly water, it can easily flow in and out of your heart and through your vessels. The path it travels is called the bloodstream.

When your body works hard, it gets hot and sweaty. Sweat is water that seeps through your skin to cool you off. The busier a body is, the more water it needs.

A busy body works hard. After a while it needs to rest. Rest lets your body heal and grow and get ready for another day.

A body that gets busy each day stays strong, healthy, and happy.

There are lots of ways to be a busy body!

Which is your favorite?

For Ken, Nicholas, and Nigel

Thanks to Annie, Alana, Sasha, Frankie, Ned, Nick, Nigel, Christopher, and Kara, for their help as advisors, assistants, or models. Thanks to my editor, Nancy Siscoe, for her valuable input, and Melanie Marin, M.D., for her expert advice.

Visit us on the Web! www.randomhouse.com/kids

Educators and librarians, for a variety of teaching tools, visit us at
www.randomhouse.com/teachers

Library of Congress Cataloging-in-Publication Data
Rockwell, Lizzy.
The busy body book : a kid's guide to fitness / Lizzy Rockwell.
p. cm.
Summary: An introduction to the human body, how it functions, and its need for exercise.
ISBN 978-0-553-11374-7 (pbk.)
1. Human body—Juvenile literature. 2. Exercise—Juvenile literature. [1. Human body. 2. Exercise.] I. Title.
QP37.R653 2008
612—dc22   2008275305

ISBN 978-0-375-82203-2 (trade) — ISBN 978-0-375-92203-9 (lib. bdg.)

MANUFACTURED IN CHINA

20 19 18 17 16 15

GETTING BUSY!

Here are some suggestions for activities that keep your body busy, healthy, and strong.

STRETCHING
(2–3 times a week)

Stretching makes your muscles flexible so you can move more easily and avoid injuries. Take your time stretching—hold each stretch for about ten seconds, relax, and then stretch again.

• *Rag Doll*—Stretches your back. From a standing position, bend over at the waist and dangle down. Let your head be heavy and your arms limp. Keep your legs slightly bent. Slooooowly roll up to standing, starting at your waist, with your head coming up last.

• *Cat and Dog*—Stretches back and neck. Get on your hands and knees with your back flat like a table. Lift your back and tuck in your chin and bottom till you look like an angry cat. Then slowly drop your stomach and lift your chin and bottom till you look like a howling dog.

• *Butterfly*—Stretches back and legs. Sit down with your knees bent so that the soles of your feet are touching and close to your body. Hold your feet and make your back as straight as possible, trying to get your knees close to the floor.

STRENGTHENING
(2–3 times a week)

These activities make your muscles stronger and your bones harder.

• *Push-aways*—For chest and arms. Stand about three feet away from the wall, facing it. Lean forward so that your outstretched arms reach the wall. Slowly bend your arms till your nose touches the wall, then slowly push away. Repeat ten times.

• *Leg Lifts*—For stomach and back muscles. Lie on your back, with your palms down by your sides. Lift your legs a few inches off the ground, keeping your back straight. Hold for five seconds, then slowly lower your legs. Repeat five times.

• *The Boat*—For back muscles. Lie on your stomach, with your arms by your hips. Lift your chin slightly off the ground. Then lift your arms up slightly, and finally lift your feet slightly, keeping your elbows and knees straight. Hold a few seconds, then release. Repeat once.

• *The Chair*—For leg muscles. Stand about a foot away from the wall, with your back to it. Bend your knees till you are in a near-sitting position, with your back pressing against the wall and most of your weight being supported by your leg muscles. Hold as long as you can.

DEEP BREATHING
(anytime you can)

Deep breathing clears your lungs and calms your mind. It's a good way to wake up in the morning or relax before going to bed.

• Flopping—Stand with your feet apart. Taking a deep breath in, raise your arms up high above your head. Swiftly fling your arms and head down toward the floor, letting your knees bend as you blow the air out of your lungs. With a deep, slow inhale, lift yourself back to the original pose, and repeat three or four times.

• Belly Breathing—Lie on your back on the floor, with your hands on your belly. Take in a deep, deep breath. Let your stomach rise up as the breath fills the bottom of your lungs first, then expands all the way up to your neck. Let the breath out slowly in the opposite way, from the top down. Squeeze your stomach so you can push every last bit of air out of your lungs before you begin the next inhale. Repeat three or four times.

MODERATE ACTIVITIES
(30 minutes or more, every day)

These are any activities, games, or chores that get your body busy. They keep you strong and healthy.

• playing tag, catch, or kickball
• sledding, snowboarding, or skiing
• bike riding or walking to school, town, or a friend's house
• hiking or climbing stairs
• raking leaves, doing housework, or carrying in groceries
• playing baseball, tennis, or football
• canoeing or kayaking
• diving or snorkeling
• playing hopscotch, hula-hooping, or swinging
• climbing a tree or a jungle gym
• playing the drums or marching with a band
• doing gymnastics, karate, dance, or cheerleading
• anything you can think of that makes your body move!

AEROBICS
(3–5 times a week, 20 or more minutes at a time)

Aerobics are energetic activities that make your lungs breathe deeply, your heart beat fast, and your skin get hot and sweaty. These activities make your heart and lungs strong and clear.

• Running; jumping rope; fast swimming; playing soccer, basketball, or ice hockey; fast bike riding; roller-skating; mountain climbing; fast uphill walking; skateboarding; and dancing

OTHER TIPS . . .

• Limit the time you spend watching TV and playing video or computer games.
• Eat well. Avoid foods high in sugar and fat. Include five servings of fruit and veggies a day.
• Be safe. Don't do anything that hurts or strains your body. Drink plenty of water. Always wear safety gear like helmets and knee and elbow pads when necessary. And remember to wear sunscreen outdoors.
• Have FUN!

Sources: The President's Council on Physical Fitness and Sports, National Association for Sport and Physical Education, *Yoga for Children* by Mary Stewart and Kathy Phillips (Simon & Schuster, 1993)

Dear Parents and Teachers,

It's easy to see that children love to move. How many times have you had to ask a child to sit still—in the car, at school, or at the dining table? Being physically active makes kids feel good. They breathe deeply, filling their lungs with energizing oxygen. They use their muscles, releasing mood-improving endorphins. Regular physical activity helps children eat well, sleep well, perform well in school, resist illness, and grow strong, cheerful, and confident.

The good news is that being physically active is natural for children. The bad news is that today many children are not active enough to stay healthy. The number of seriously overweight children in the United States has tripled in the past twenty years. Obesity is linked to other serious health risks such as diabetes, heart disease, osteoporosis, and depression. While diet plays a major role in our children's health, physical activity is an equally important factor. Surveys show that as many as half of our children do not get even a moderate (30 minutes a day, five days a week) amount of exercise. Yet they now spend an average of four hours a day in front of the TV or computer. Even children who do not gain weight easily are often not active enough to keep their heart, lungs, bones, and muscles in good condition. By giving our children education and positive guidance, we take the first steps in breaking this pattern.

When children know about the remarkable potential of their bodies, they want to test it out. When they see others engaged in activities that look fun and stimulating, they want to join in. As parents and educators, we can set examples of healthy living by making changes in our own habits. Small lifestyle adjustments can communicate that fitness is a priority. We can walk to school or the store, set limits on sedentary activities, take the stairs instead of the elevator. In *The Busy Body Book,* I have chosen friendly, encouraging words and images that I hope will inspire children to make their own good choices. This book is for the competitive athlete as well as the contemplative artist. I hope that all children will find themselves in its pages, feel proud of their bodies, and be inspired to move. Physical activity is natural for all of us. So let's get busy and have some fun!

With warm wishes,
Lizzy Rockwell